〖SPOTS〗

SPOTS...a guide to rideable uk architecture by Harry Bastard

first edition 2001 © Harry Bastard.
ISBN: 0-9541454-0-2

Published by

WJ&T publishing
50 Providence place
Brighton BN1 4GE
England.

Printed by

Chandlers print
Saxon mews, Reginald rd
Bexhill-on-sea
East sussex
TN39 3PJ

*All enquiries and post related to this guide send to:

Spots, PO Box 84
Brighton
BN1 4WS

Illustrations & maps by  Mark Hooley & KREM 4 THE DEPARTMENT....

The publishers and author have done their best to ensure the accuracy
of all the information in *spots a guide to uk rideable architecture*
however, they can accept no responsibility for any loss, injury,
or inconvenience sustained by any person as a result of information
or advice contained in this guide.

Whilst this guide represents objects suitable for the useage of in ways other
than their original design intends this also means that this
inventive usage of the aforementioned architecture might possibly
cause offence, be illegal or be not allowed for other reasons.
the publishers and author can accept no responsibilty for any legal
actions or similar resulting from information obtained from within this
spots a guide to uk rideable architecture-
all actions are solely the responsibility of the practitioner.

[THE LITTLE BIT OF WRITING AT THE FRONT[]

AS EVERYONE ALREADY KNOWS SKATEBOARDING IS A HIDEOUS CRIME
OF SELF GRATIFICATION AND MUST NOT BE ENCOURAGED IN ANY WAY
FOR THE SOULS OF OUR CHILDREN ARE AT STAKE. WALLS ARE FOR
HOLDING UP BUILDINGS STEPS ARE FOR WALKING ON AND WHAT THE
FUCK IS A BANK FOR[]ALSO ITS REALLY ANNOYING THAT PEOPLE CAN
ENJOY THEMSELVES WITH SO LITTLE AND WE CANT MAKE ANY MONEY
OUT OF IT[]. NOTHING POSITIVE WILL EVER COME FROM IT STOP NOW AND
DO SOMETHING WE WANT YOU TO.

THE WEIRDEST THING IS THAT WAS IT A SKATEBOARD THAT MADE IT
POSSIBLE FOR ME TO DO THIS OR JUST THE GENERAL ATTITUDE OF
SKATEBOARDERS. THE LATTER I THINK AND IM HOPING THAT THIS GUIDE
GETS PEOPLE TRAVELLING MORE AND MEETING NEW PEOPLE BECAUSE I
HAVE TO SAY THAT IT IS ONE OF THE BEST THINGS YOU CAN DO WITH YOUR
LIFE ALSO IT WILL HOPEFULLY LEAD TO MORE PEOPLE GETTING TOGETHER
AND MAYBE VOICING AN OPINION WHEN NEEDED []YOU HAVE A RIGHT TO BE
HEARD[].

A BROKEN ANKLE MADE ME FINALLY DECIDE TO MAKE WHAT YOU ARE ABOUT
TO CONSUME WITH YOUR EYES. IT TOOK ME TWO YEARS AND A MINISCULE
BUDGET TO TRAVEL PHOTO AND MEET EVERYONE AND EVERYTHING WITHIN
THE NEXT FEW HUNDREDS PAGES. YOUR HOPEFULLY GOING TO FIND THIS
GUIDE INTERESTING IN SOME WAY OR OTHER BUT IF NOT THEN PLEASE WRITE
IN COZ IM NOT ON A ONE MAN MISSION HERE I NEED INPUT AND FROM AS
MANY PEOPLE AS POSSIBLE.

OBVIOUSLY IVE MISSED SOME PEOPLES FACES OUT SPOTS CITIES AND SOME
OTHER THINGS THAT WERENT VISIBLE UNTIL I WAS FINISHED BUT THATS THE
WAY IT IS. LEARN FROM YOUR MISTAKES AND MOST IMPORTANTLY ALWAYS
LEAVE EVERYTHING TILL THE LAST MINUTE YOU CANT GO WRONG.

X MARKS THE SHOP.......

⬜CONTENTS⬜

⬜SCOTLAND⬜
ABERDEEN
DUNDEE
EDINGBURGH
LIVINGSTONE
GLASGOW
OTHER SCOTLAND
⬜THE NORTH⬜
NEWCASTLE
MIDDLESBOROUGH
LEEDS
LIVERPOOL
MANCHESTER
SHEFFIELD
⬜THE MIDLANDS⬜
BIRMINGHAM
NOTTINGHAM
LEICESTER
MILTON KEYNES
⬜WALES⬜
NEWPORT

CARDIFF
BRIDGEND
SWANSEA
⬜N. IRELAND⬜
BELFAST
⬜THE SOUTH⬜
BRISTOL
OXFORD
NORWICH
IPSWICH
HARROW
LONDON
BRIGHTON
PORTSMOUTH
SOUTHAMPTON
PLYMOUTH
PENZANCE
OTHER SOUTH
SKATEPARKS
REPLY
CHEERS

SCOTLAND

B.WESTBURN
MINI

C.DENBURN
BANKS

F.BROAD STREET BLOCKS.STEPS N STUFF

01

STREET SKATE SNOW

EFFECTIVE EDGE

EFFECTIVE EDGE

EFFECTIVE EDGE

212A PERTH ROAD, DUNDEE
(01382) 221 155
WWW.EFFECTIVEEDGE.CO.UK

BANG!

WE WANT YOU
TO THINK MORE

UNABOMBER SKATEBOARDS 0044 (0)121 2122115

⬛MEETING PLACE⬛

⬛LOADS OF MAD STUFF⬛

⬛OTHER SPOTS NOT SHOWN⬛

D.CAR PARK BANK 2 WALL⬛DRY⬛
E.MACK BANKS
F&I.DOWNHILL MADNESS
G.BIG METAL GIRDER
H.FLAT BANK⬛BARS N STUFF⬛
J.BUS STATION STEPS

B. BRISTO BANKS

CLOTHIAN ROAD RAIL

CLOTHIAN LEDGE

K. CINEMA BLOCKS

K. WEIRD BANK THIN

vaughan baker

f.s.u

HE WHO
CREATES
A BRIGHT
AND
FLAMING
SPARK
MUST HAVE
WITHIN HIM
A CRAZY
DEMON

nietsche

LIVING

BRITS
OUT

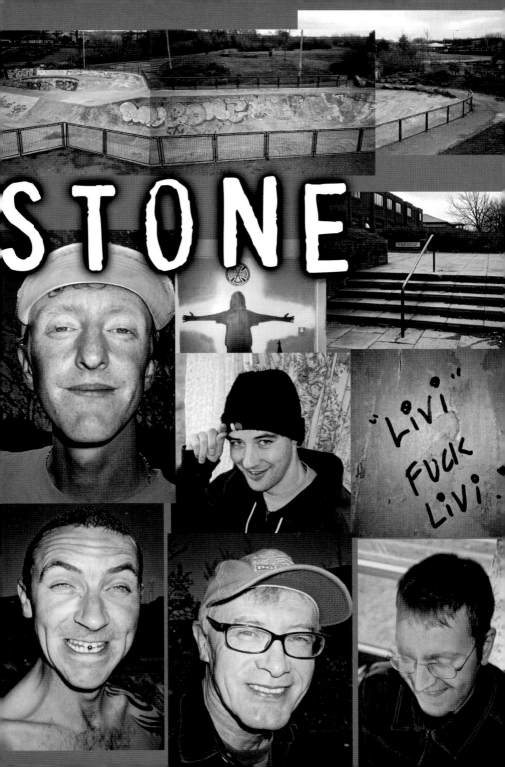

STONE

"Livi"
Fuck
Livi"

GLAS

DON'T

A.UNDERPASS

D.ST GEORGES SQUARE

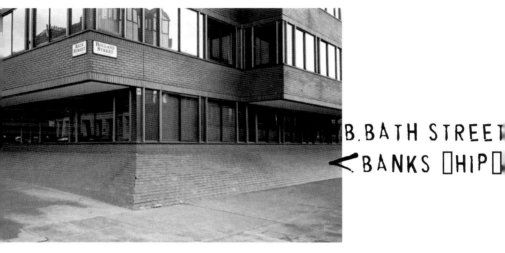

B.BATH STREET
< BANKS []HIP[]

> F.MITCHELL
AND RAILS

GLASGOW

TRIBAL JUNKI
- TACTICAL JEANS UNIT -

mail order/wholesale tel 00 44 (0)141 552 7078

G.GOMA[ALL THIS AREA IS NICE & OPEN]

J.MOD BANKS

GARNETT HILL R.I.P   EASTER BANKS R.I.P

[OTHER SPOTS NOT SHOWN
C.BUCHANAN ST[MADNESS
D.ST GEORGES KICKER

H.CALEDONIAN STEPS N THAT

STERLING □ KINGS PARK □

MONKEY

OTHER

ARBROATH

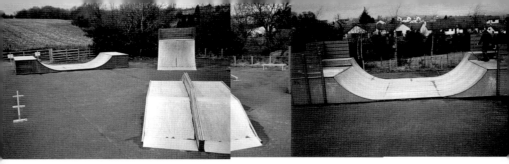

K I P P E N

SCOTLAND

THE SKATE INN

PERTH MINI (NEAR PRISON)

AdioFootwear
UKTeam2001

Left to Right:
Nick**Warman** (Team Manager)
Danny**McCourt**
Sam**Culshaw**
Adam**Fletcher**
Craig**Smedley**
Nick**Marker**
Mark**Burrows**

Not Pictured:
Dan**Rees**
Sam**Jefferies**

Photo:**MikeWright**

Duogy **Mclaughlan** ▪ Bruce ▪ Howard **Cooke** ▪ Bruce

THE NORTH

nsc

ZOO YORK. ETNIES. ES. EMERICA.
DC SHOE CO. DOPE. DROORS.
OSIRIS. WEST BEACH. SPLIT.
GIRL. CHOCOLATE CIRCA.
JANSPORT. THE NORTH. SERIAL
KILLER. PORNSTAR HOOK UPS.
BLIND. WORLD INDUSTRIES. NIXON.
FOURSQUARE. SESSIONS.
SPECIAL BLEND.

NY FITTED CAPS IN EVERY SIZE.
EVERY COLOUR.

NSC - STOCKISTS OF SKATE BOARDS, SNOWBOARDS,
ROLLER BLADES & ICE HOCKEY EQUIPMENT.
NEWCASTLE'S PREMIER SKATE STORE-SKATE OWNED AND RAN.
SUPPORT YOUR LOCAL SKATE SHOP!

16 SHAKESPEARE STREET. NEWCASTLE UPON TYNE. NE1 6AQ. T:0191 230 2595

NEWO

B. HAYMARKET BLOCKS

C. CIVIC CENTRE

E. UNIVERSITY

D....

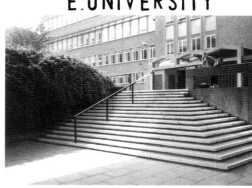

E...

& E.... AGAIN

NEWCASTLE

G.BANK □STEPS AT END□

I.QUEENS BANK

<H..

J..>

K.SMALL MEDIUM & LARGE

∧
K.FIVE BRIDGES

☐SPOTS NOT SHOWN☐
A.MONUMENT PLATFORM
F.POLYTECHNIC

Heroin Skateboards.

HUGE
in Burnley

Also doing pretty good in Osaka, Tokyo, Kyoto, Accrington, Bolton, Rochdale, Ramsbottom, Darlington, Myrabakken, Sheffield, Brighton, Wallasey, New Cross, Blackburn, Leeds, Blackpool, Manchester, Morcambe, Grange Over Sands, Garstang, Kidderminster, Norwich, Birmingham, Penzance, Dundee, Aberdeen, Edinburgh, Gospor Swansea, Acle, Stockwell, Hasligden, Worthing , Mosley Hill, Allerton, Lancaster, New Milton, Brockenhurst, Blackheath, Greenwich, Wimbledon, Hebden Bridge and Chichester.

Look Out for the ne

nosebleed concave.

wer Distribution 020 8861 0070

available on selected model

Mischief
SkateStore.
5RegencyWestMall,Stockton-on-Tees
P. 01642 608400
www.mischiefskatestore.com
PeterSingh.SwitchHeelflip.

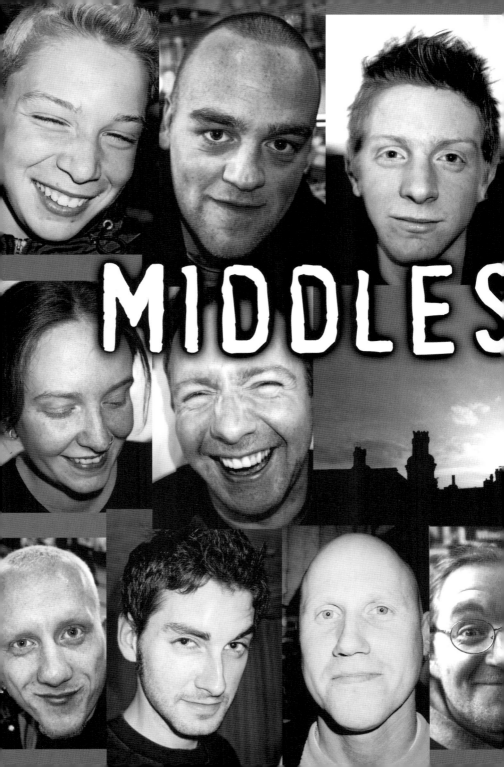

MIDDLES

A. THE BOULEVARD

∧ A. THE BOULEVARD ∧

⬚MEETING PLACE⬚
V

A. CIVIC STEPS ∧

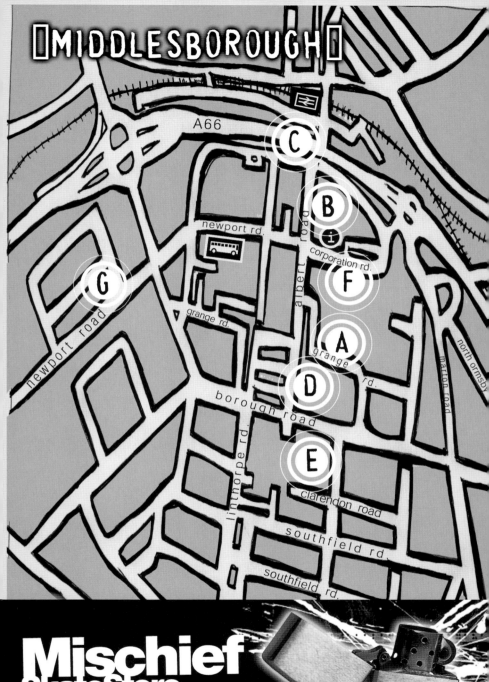

BOROUGH

F. SOME LITTLE BANKS

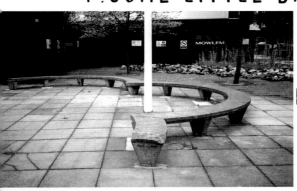

F. CURVY BENCHE

∧ B. ALBERT BRIDGE STUFF ∧

C. GAP TO ROAD
OR OVER THE BAR
IF YOUR FEELING
< FRISKY

D.LOOKS GOOD EH?

12 YEAR OLD BENCH

E.UNI BUILDINGS

G.CANNON PARK

THE FUTURES BRIGHT

LEE

A.PLAYHOUSE☐MEETING ☐PLACE☐

B.PIG AND WHISTLE

C.THE TECH RAILS AND BLOCK

D.BUSINESS CENTR
POSSIBLE HIP
[GET SOME WOOD[

K.THE UNI

∧

THE UNI 7

LOADS MORE

TUFF□ >

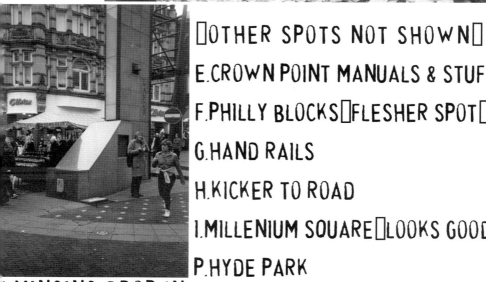

□OTHER SPOTS NOT SHOWN□

E. CROWN POINT MANUALS & STUFF

F. PHILLY BLOCKS□FLESHER SPOT□

G. HAND RAILS

H. KICKER TO ROAD

I. MILLENIUM SQUARE□LOOKS GOOD□

P. HYDE PARK

J. MINGING DROP IN

PAUL SILVESTER
SWITCH KICKFLIP
LEEDS UNIVERSITY

DuFFS®

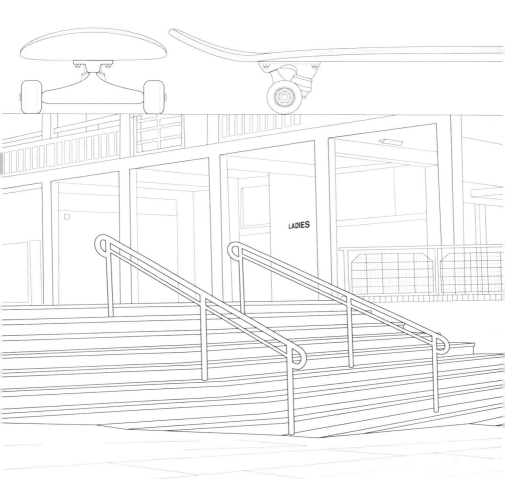

LADIES

DOCUMENT SKATEBOARD MAGAZINE
VIEWING THINGS DIFFERENTLY

▶ UNIT 17 TEMPLAR HOUSE TEMPLAR WAY BRISTOL BS1 6GH ENGLAND TEL: 0117 929 3060 E-MAIL: document@4130.com

LIVER

A. THE COURTS HANDRAILS

B. THE HEX

C. PIER HEAD

E. ECHOES

G. H GROUND IT

LIVERPOOL

WHO NEEDS SKATE SPOTS ?

fig. 1

fig. 2

fig. 3

POOL

H. LITTLEWOODS

I. THE CHEESE

[MEETING PLACE]

L. BOLD ST DOUBL

M.POST OFFICE BANKS

O.DOCK
ROAD
BANKS
V

P.POLICE BANKS

O.WHITE RAIL

[OTHER SPOTS NOT SHOWN]
F.MOORFIELDS DOUBLE FLIGHT
J.LIME STREET STEPS
K.ST JOHNS HANDRAILS
N.UNIVERSITY BANKS

UK RIDERS:
ANDY SIMPSON
DAVE CHESSON

ANDY SIMPSON

ROOKIE**NYC**
SKATE OF MINE

DISTRIBUTED IN THE U.K. BY:
PROJECTS DISTRIBUTION LTD.
UNIT 28, TEMPLAR HOUSE
TEMPLE WAY, BRISTOL BS1 6H
TEL: 0117 925 1025
FAX: 0117 925 1026
www.info@projectskate.com

keith miller
andy scott
mike sutcliffe
james ewans

wisdom **mcr**
unit 4 afflecks arcade
oldham street
manchester
england

01618323192

MANCH

A.UNIVERSITY [LOADS MORE STUFF]

B.UNI BANKS   D.GASWORKS

D.GASWORKS BAD ASS GAP

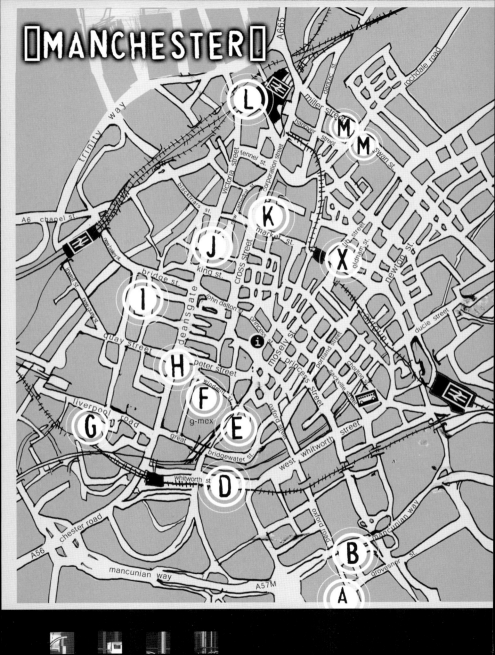

ESTER

E.BRIDGEWATER HALL

£250,000!

F.GMEX [BLIND BUMPS]

G.CASTLEFIELD ARENA

G.THE RAIL IN THE MIDDLE

I.BANK BLOCK THINGS

I.BIG DOUBLE

J.METAL BENCHES

J.CONCRETE ONES

K.M&S LEDGES WITH GAPS

L.VICTORIA TRAIN STATION STUFF

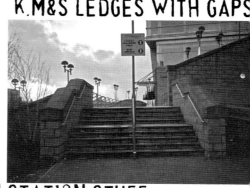

M.COOP STEPS & NASTY GAP TO LEDGE
[SPOTS NOT SHOWN] B.THE KERBS[DRY] H.NORTHERN SQUARE BLOCKS.

headstrong

www.headstrong.co.uk

OTHER BRANDS INCLUDE:-

ALIEN, BLIND, CHOCOLATE, DARKSTAR, DROORS, ELEMENT, FOURSTAR, GIRL, PIG, SHORTYS, SPITFIRE, TOY MACHINE, ZERO, FSU, GANGSTAR, NYLON, ONCUS, REACTION, SPUNKY.....

www.headstrong.co.uk

CHECKOUT THE SITE FOR FREE STUFF, FREE COMPETITIONS AND SPECIAL OFFERS. AVAILIBLE 24/7.

e-mail us: sales@headstrong.co.uk

OR CALL 0870 900 80 55

calls charged at national rate

SHEF

B.LEDGE INNIT

B.THE CRUCIBLE BLOCKS & LEDGES N STUF

C.THE SHIPPO HIP

financial assassinations.

GIW™

SPOTS NOT SHOWN
A. THE HUMP
D. HILLS
E. BANKS AND BARS
F. WOODY HANDRAIL

J. COURT LEDGES

G. FIRESTATION THINGS   H. BUS STATION

I. THE PARK

THE MIDLANDS

ippin' gap:ben blake~photo:leo sharp

THE MIDLANDS FAVOURITE
IDEALBIRMINGHAM
EL:0121 236 3900 FAX:0121 236 6345

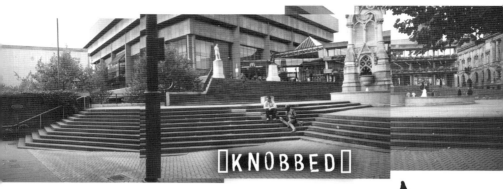

[KNOBBED]

V B.CENTRAL LIBRARY ^

KNOBBED[

F.LEDGE GAP TO ROAD

[KNOBBED[

E.CENTRAL TV

NGHAM

. CENTENARY SQUARE

. CHURCH ST BANKS

J. LONG MARBLE LEDGE

∧ N. UNIVERSITY LOADS OF STUFF ∧

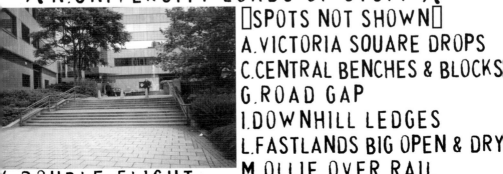

K. DOUBLE FLIGHT

◻SPOTS NOT SHOWN◻
A. VICTORIA SQUARE DROPS
C. CENTRAL BENCHES & BLOCKS
G. ROAD GAP
I. DOWNHILL LEDGES
L. FASTLANDS BIG OPEN & DRY
M. OLLIE OVER RAIL

NONSTOP SPORT > INFORMATION > # 0115 953-1002 > ADDRESS: 14 ST. JAMES
_STREET, NOTTINGHAM NG1 6FG > EMAIL: nonstop.sport@virgin.n
> FAX: 0115 947-5886 > NOTTINGHAM'S OLDEST SKATE STORE > est. 19

NOTT

C. POLY BANKS

.BLOCKS & DROPS

E. AMPITHEATRE

□NOTTINGHAM□

G. HOCKLEY BANKS

K. DOWNHILL RUN UP

J. WORSE THAN THEY LO

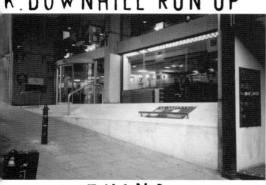

L. THING

M. SMALLER ONES ASWE

O. ☐MAPLE STREET MINI☐
ANOTHER AMAZING
COUNCIL CONTRIBUTION
TO THE SKATEBOARD
COMMUNITY. 8FT WIDE
METAL & SOME VERT

N. THEATRE STUFF >

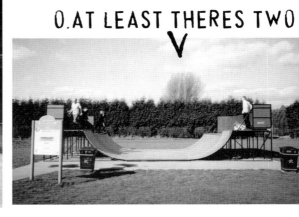

O. AT LEAST THERES TWO
V

YOU FIND IT

P. FOREST RAIL

[OTHER SPOTS NOT SHOWN]

B. BANKS & DOUBLE FLIGHT IN SUBWAY

D. THE BUS STATION

I. THE PARK DOWNHILLS

LEICESTER'S NO.1 SKATESHOP

22 MALCOLM ARCADE, LEICESTER
PHONE 0116 2516362
CONTACT@CASINOSKATES.COM
WWW.CASINOSKATES.COM

∧

A.THIS IS

ALL THE

UNIVERSITY

∨

B. ITS A LEDGE THAT LOOKS GOOD

C. DOUBLE FLIGHT

H. HIGH PAINTED LEDG

I. THE QUAY

K.DOUBLE FLIGHT   J.THE TRIANGLES

MILES OUT OF TOWN

[SPOTS NOT SHOWN]

D.DOWNHILL LEDGES

E.LAW COURTS GAP

F.UNDERCOVER STEPS

G.MANUAL PADS

L.DOUBLE FLIGHT

M.PHEONIX CURBS

VICTORIA PARK GOOD HIP

WAYNE'S
POODLE
PARLOU

MILTON

BATHING
PROHIBITED

Pedestrians do no

P. THE TRAIN STATION

A. MAD BLOCKS AND STEPS

B. BLIND BUMPS AT TOP

D. MASSIVE DOUBLE FLIGHT AND LEDGE

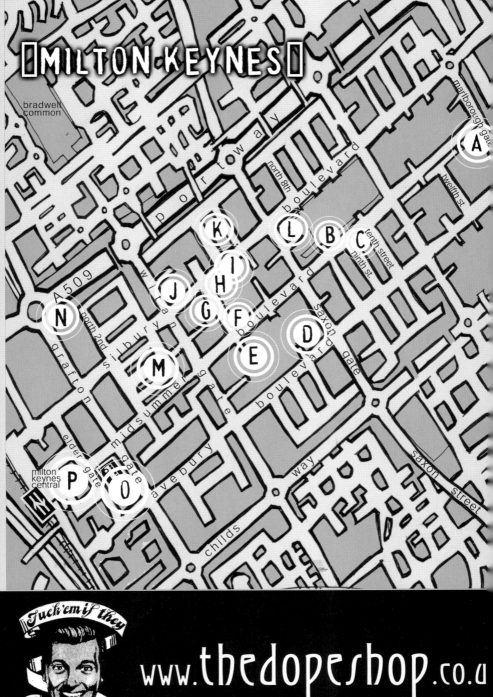

KEYNES

To Whom It May Concern:

Please do not leave
your underwear here !

It is not a laundry!!!
Thank you

e Priority

P. THE TRAIN STATION

C. CURVY BLOCK

D. ANOTHER BLOCK

D. STEPS N RAILS

E. STAIR ASSISTANCE DEVIC

F. LITTLE LEDGES

H. BIG GAP OVER RAI

G.THE BEIGE STEPS

I.LITTLE GAP OVER RAIL

G.THE BEIGE GAP THING

K.NICE FLAT BARS

N.OTHER STUFF ASWELL

ESE ARE EVERYWHERE

[SPOTS NOT SHOWN]
J.HANDRAILS
L.M&S BLOCKS
M.KNOBBED LEDGE
O.THE BUS STATION STUFF

WALES

Freestyle Skate Store

Simon Hacket

Josh Perret

Barry Jenkins

Dan Wood

Lee Dainton

Matt Davies

Saul (Hate) Evans

Dan Cates

ZOOPORT
Wales

Mail Order 01633 213129
www.freestyleskates.co.uk

A. COLLEGE BANKS

B. BARRACK HILL

NEARLY TRANNY

G. PIG BANKS

I. ANOTHER COUNCIL EFFORT

☐NEWPORT☐

FREESTYLE
SKATE STORE

NEWPORT   01633 21312

PORT

SKATE EXTREME

J.FAIRWATER SHOPS K.DANGEROUS THINGS

J.CWYMBRAN SHOPPIN CENTRE

]SPOTS NOT SHOWN[
.ST DAVIDS HIP   D.KINGSWAY CENTRE HANDRAIL
.GOLD TOPS DROPS & STUFF   H.WIMPY STEPS & BAN

CAR[

A. TRAIN STATION

B. BUTE SQUARE

E. MILLENIUM SQUARE

D. RED BANKS

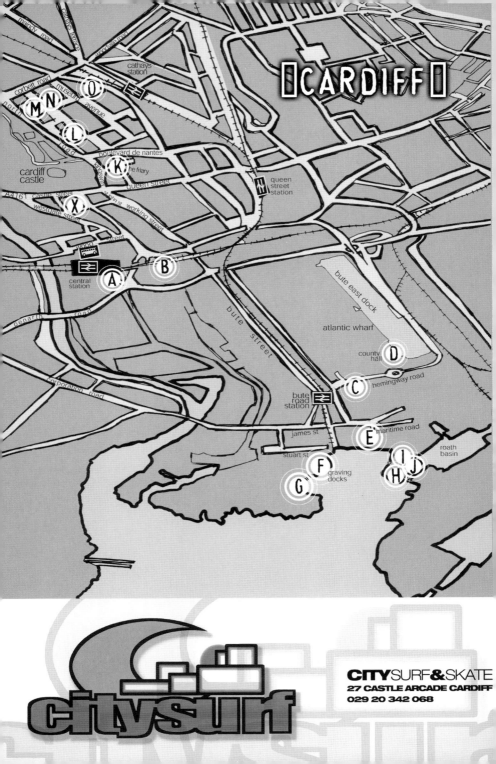

IFF

. ☐MEETING SPOT☐   F. LOADS OF THESE

E. AGAIN

D. TIGHT TRANNY   C. UCI BENCHES

F. SPORTS CAFE STEPS

I. MARBLE BENCHES

J. PORK CHOP

K. MONUMEN

K. MONUMENT LEDGE

K. GOOD LAUGH

M.GAP OVER STEPS

N.WELSH OFFICE

N.WELSH 2 WALL

N.WELSH LEDGE

O.DOUBLE KINK

[SPOTS NOT SHOWN]
G. SC BENCHES
H.NORWEGIAN CHURCH
PLATFORMS N THAT
L.GAP OVER CHAIN

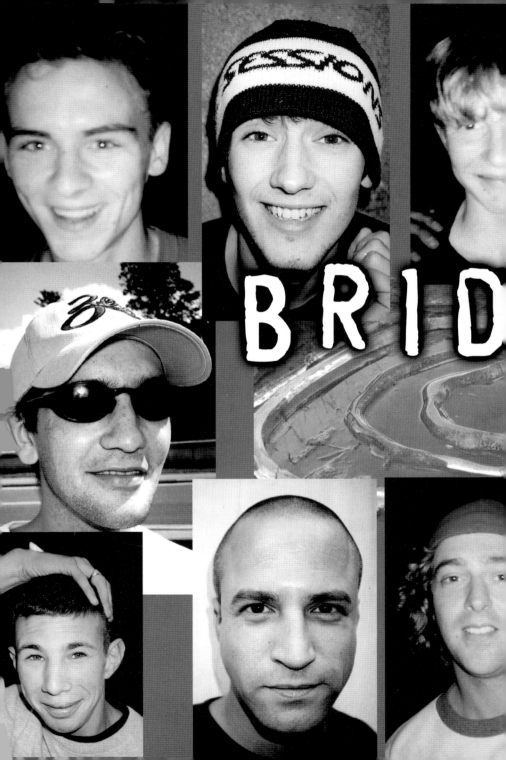

B.HANDRAIL

B.YMCA DOUBLE FLIGHT

.CARPARK LEDGE THING

C.CARPARK BLOCKS

E. BT GAP

D.FOODCHAIN

E. BT LEDGE N STEPS

LOADS EVERYWHERE

E. BOF GAP

H. WALL 2 RAIL

H. STEPS AND RAIL STUFF

[SPOTS NOT SHOWN]

A. SK8 PARK

G. YC PLASTICS GOOD SPOT WITH LOADS OF STUFF

Daniel Joyce. Died: Age 1 month.

SWAN

How to be a
scatterbrain

A.CASTLE GARDENS

A.CURVY WALLS

A.LITTLE LEDGE

A.BIG LEDGE

A.DOUBLE KINK

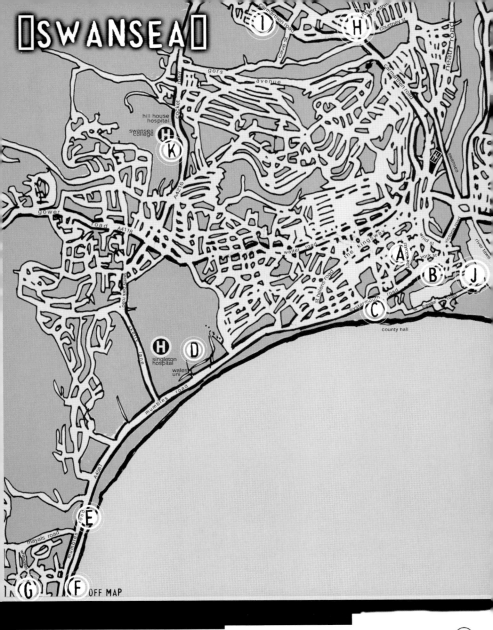

ou let your
eel your
bs?

Skateboarder
magazine

EXSPORTS

SKate
boards
from
£15

STOCK
MUST
GO

SEA

A. THE
OTHER
HALF

C. COUNTY HALL [NIGHT TIME]

D. PHONE IN SICK

D. LOADS OF STEPS

D. GAP LEDGE THING

D. SHORT RUN UP

F. THE KNAB

F. UP OR DOWN?

G. MUMBOS RAIL

G. MUMBOS DOUBL

[SPOTS NOT SHOWN]

B. CRAP SK8 PARK   I. INDOOR PARK

E. BLACK PILL MINI   J. STAIRS & RAILS

H. BANK ON ROOF   K. GNARLY RAIL

BOB SANDERSON·BEN BLAKE

NORMAN WYNTER·RICH LEWIS·JOHN FISHER

III
a third foot

MIXED & SERVED IN ENGLAND

DAMON LEVANTHAL·TED MOYLE

NORTHERN
IRELAND

all city:skater owned
31   queen   street
#[028] 9031 9465

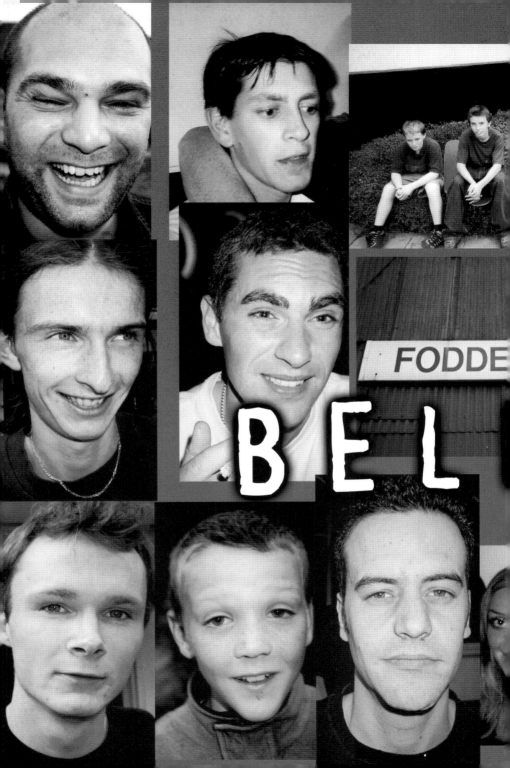

FODDE

BEL

VICTORIA BANK 2 WALL C.VICTORIA HANDRAIL

D.QUEENS UNI LEDGES   D.SOME STAIRS

E.STUDENT UNION THINGY   E.STUDENT UNION RAILS

H.EUROPA RAILS

J.WATERFRONT STEPS

J.WATERFRONT BENCHES

J.WALLIE THING

J.LEDGE

.MORE STEPS

〔SPOTS NOT SHOWN〕 >

A.ST BRIDES BENCHES
B.THE GAP

F.HOSPITAL RAILS AND STUFF
G.BOTANIC BANK
I.ST ANNES NEW STUFF
K.NEW YORK〔UNDERCOVER〕
L.GASWORKS BENCHES

HESHMAN!

Geoff Rowley
H·K·D

Exclusive UK Distributor; Shiner Ltd., Lawrence Hill, Bristol BS5 9JB. Tel: 0117 955 6035. e-mail info@shiner.co.uk

THE SOUTH

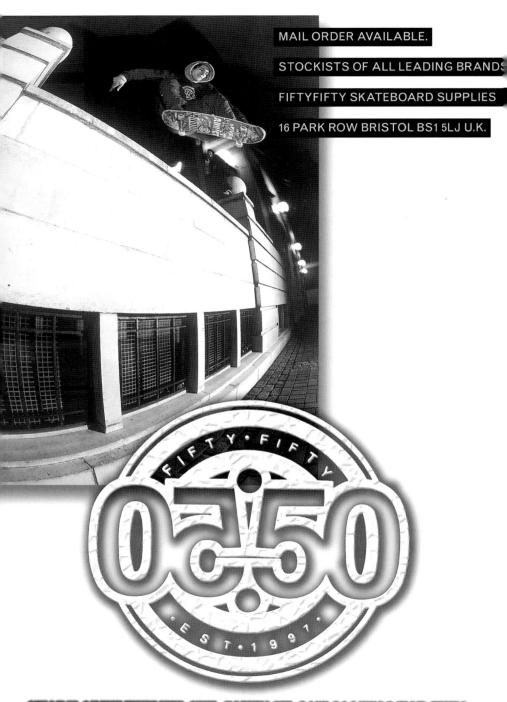

A. SUNLIFE ⬚MORE THAN THIS⬚

C.LLOYDS

.SPECTRUM STEPS

.BEDMINSTER

STORE OPEN TEN TIL SIX.
CONTACT: 0117 914 7783 FOR INFO

.LITTLE LLOYDS HIP & BAR[]TOP BLOCK KNOBBED[]

C.LLOYDS ∧

< D.LOOKS LIKE HANDRAILS

[]SPOTS NOT SHOWN[]

E.COLLEGE GREEN
[]GOOD MEETING SPOT[

G.BANK TO RAIL

H.BEDMINSTER

Danny Wainwright

SS20 HAS BEEN BASED IN OXFORD FOR THE PAST 12 YEARS. THE SHOP IS R
AND OWNED BY SKATEBOARDERS FOR SKATEBOARDERS. UNLIKE SOME OTH
SKATESHOPS WHICH WE WON'T CARE TO MENTION, WE ACTUALLY KNOW H
SKATEBOARDS WORK. WE EVEN KNOW HOW TO PUT GRIPTAPE ON A BOARD
CAN DO SO RIGHT IN FRONT OF YOUR EYES. WE HAVE SUPPORTED THE SPO
WHICH WE LOVE FOR MORE THAN 12 YEARS, AND DURING THAT TIME WE HA
SPONSORED MANY LOCAL SKATERS AND STILL CONTINUE TO DO SO. THOS
SKATERS HAVE INCLUDING DANNY WAINWRIGHT, ALEX MOUL AND TOM PEN
WE'VE HEARD THAT THOSE GUYS ARE QUITE GOOD NOWADAYS! ONE OF OU
OWNERS WAS RECENTLY INVITED TO THE LEGENDS SERIES COMPETITION A
MUNSTER, AND WOUND UP WITH A PLACE ON THE PODIUM. NOT SURE HOW
MANY OTHER SKATESHOP OWNERS CAN CLAIM THE SAME? WE ALSO HAVE
SKATEPARK DOWN THE ROAD BUILT BY THE OXFORD WHEELS PROJECT, A LO
CHARITY SET UP AN RUN BY AN SS20 OWNER. HOW MANY SKATESHOP
OWNERS CAN HONESTLY SAY THAT THEY HAVE PUT AS MUCH TIME AND EFFO
INTO HELPING THEIR LOCAL SKATE COMMUNITY. ALL OF OUR STAFF SKATE
SOME ARE VERY GOOD, OTHERS ARE NOT. IT DOESN'T MATTER, WE ALL HAVE
NONE THE LESS. WE STOCK JUST ABOUT EVERY SKATEBOARD BRAND ON T
MARKET, INCLUDING ALL THE USEFUL, BUT NOT FASHIONABLE ITEMS THAT Y
MIGHT NEED (YOU TRY FINDING A REPLACEMENT FURY PIVOT CUP IN YOU
LOCAL SKATE/FASHION STORE). WE 'VE SEEN SKATEBOARDING GO THROUG
MANY BOOMS AND LOWS DURING THE TIME WE'VE BEEN HERE, AND WITH YO
SUPPORT HOPE THAT WE CAN SEE IT THROUGH A FEW MORE. IF YOU DO US
THIS BOOK AND COME TO VISIT OXFORD, STOP BY AND SEE US. WE MIGHT
YOU IN ON A FEW MORE LOCAL SPOTS. HAVE A SAFE JOURNEY. CHEERS, SS2

A. BROAD STREET

B. LIBRARY STEPS N THA

. VIROLOGY BANKS N RAILS

E. CASTLE MOUND

H. SHOE LANE DROP IN

SPOTS NOT SHOWN☐
ZOOLOGY STEPS & LEDGES
ST EBBES BENCHES & BLOCKS
HINKSEY PADDLING POOL

F. DOUBLE FLIGHT

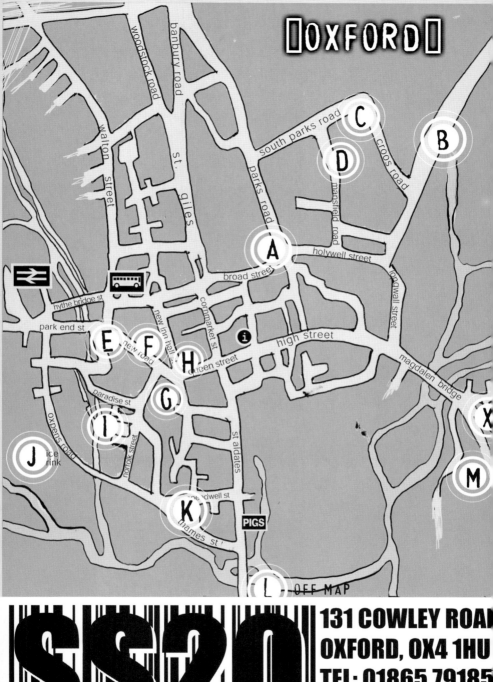

OXFORD

woodstock road · banbury road · walton street · st. giles · parks road · south parks road · cross road

C · B · D · mansfield road · A · holywell street · longwall street · broad street · cornmarket st · i · high street · magdalen bridge

hythe bridge st · park end st · new inn hall st · new road · E · F · H · queen street · G · paradise st · oxpens road · I · norfolk street · J · ice rink · st aldates · broad well st · X · M · K · thames st · PIGS · L — OFF MAP

SS20

MONDAY-SAT 10am-6pm · SUNDAYS 11am-4pm

**131 COWLEY ROAD
OXFORD, OX4 1HU
TEL: 01865 79185
SHOP@SS20.COM
WWW.SS20.COM**

I. COLLEGE RAILS

K. BANK 2 WALL

J. ICE RINK STUFF

M. TURN RIGHT ON JACKDAW LANE

UK SKATEBOARD MAGAZINE

Sidewalk

TOM PENNY FIGHTS OFF SATAN'S TAUNTS WITH A HUGE POP SHOVE IN FRANCE: PHOTO: BARTOK.

"a bored mind makes an ideal office for the devil"

EVERYMONTHINSKATESHOPS

DO YOU FEEL
RIPPED OFF
BECAUSE THIS
PAGE IS BLANK

an morris gary simmonds chris stauff

an hearne peter adam sandy car

FEDERAL

WWW.FEDERALBIKES.COM
SPARKYS DISTRIBUTION

01424 718172   01424 718168
407 599 7257   407 599 7259

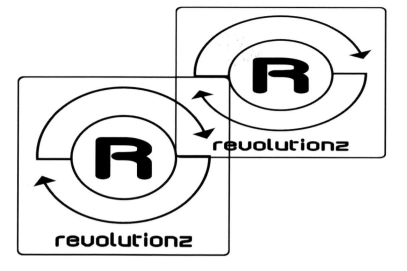

FREEDOM TO EXPRESS

it may not be revolutionary thinking
but it sure beats the crap
out of most things...

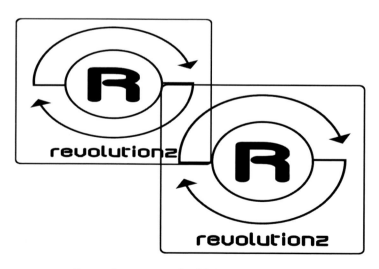

25, timber hill norwich NR1 3JZ
www.revolutionz.co.uk

NOR

.BUS STATION GAP

B.HANDRAIL

C.GAP THING

C.BIG STEPS

E.HANDRAIL

F.MARKET STEPS N BENCHE

NORWICH

barrack st · st crispins road · oak st. · st crispins road · duke street · colegate · oak street · duke street · st georges street · st andrews st · palace street · lower close · upper close · potergate · lobster lane · bedford street · prince of wales road · st giles street · bethel st · rose lane · king street · rose lane · theatre street · chapelfield east · castlemarket street · rouen road · chapelfield road · st stephens street · surrey st · all saints green · ber street · queens road

revolutionz

skate snowboard bmx

there is a serious alternative
visit dave and james

25, timber hill, norwich NR1 3JZ

www.revolutionz.co.uk

01603 629313

WICH

TOWN HALL RAILS

J.NEW YORK BANKS

K.DROP IN

N.LAW COURTS

ANGLIA SQUARE

[SPOTS NOT SHOWN]
A.XTREME FUN SK8 PARK
H.FORUM[IN BUILDING]
I.MANUAL PAD
L.FLAT BARS
M.FLAT BARS

RUDE 69

ude Rider: Ben Jones / Photo: Shawn Allen
www.rudeonline.com

R.U.D.E.
Street Skate Snow

IP41BD. Tel: 01473 230573

7 Orwell place , Ipswich , Suffolk IP41BD. Tel: 01473 230573

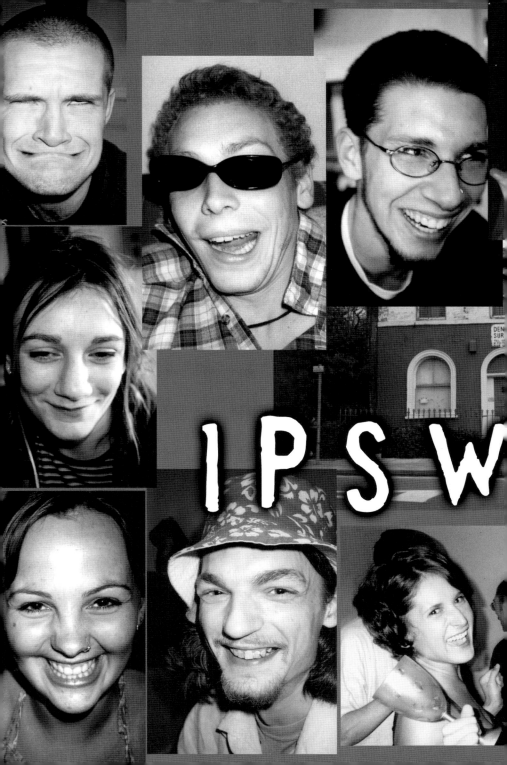

A. CROWN POOLS

A. CROWN POOLS

B. WHITE BLOCKS

C. WOLSEY DOUBLE

.STAIRS & LEDGE

E. COURT LEDGES

⬜IPSWICH⬜

R.U.D.E.

Street Skate Snow

17 Orwell place , Ipswich , Suffolk IP41BD. Tel: 01473 230573

ICH

G.BLUE BARS

J.COLLEGE

J.THINGY

J.STEPS N LEDGE

I.DROP IN

[SPOTS NOT SHOWN]
F.CROMWELL SQUARE
[MEETING SPOT]
H.SKATEPARK TO BE BUILT

MORE ^
POSITIVE
REINFORCEMENT

DEATH
SKATEBOARDS

C.FLOWER POT

E.HANDRAIL

E.LEDGES

F.STEEP BANK

G.HARROW PARK

FIND DAN CATES
TO SKATE THIS
<

Instant Criminal,
just add skateboard!

H.SILVER RAILS   H.THING

I.2 OF THESE   J.A NASTY BANK

G.HARROW PARK

]SPOTS NOT SHOWN[]

A.BESBOROUGH BLOCKS   D.GROVE HILL DOWNHILLS

B.ROAD GAPS[]UNDERCOVER[] K.DOUBLE KINK LEDGE

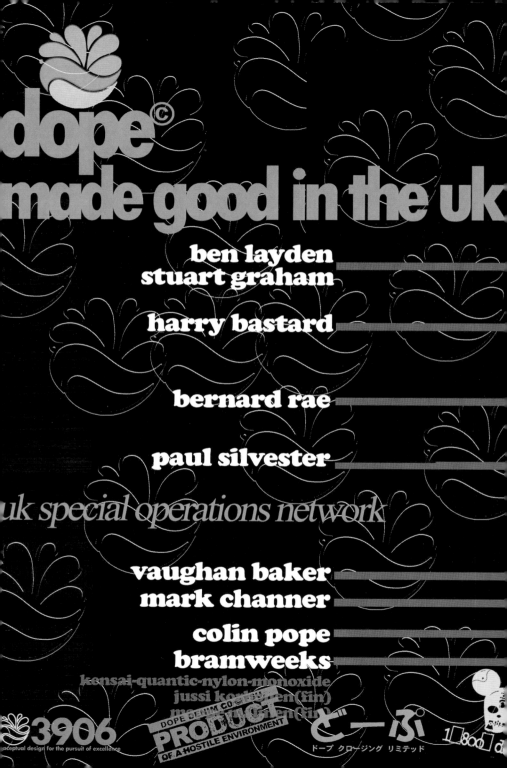

dope©
made good in the uk

ben layden
stuart graham

harry bastard

bernard rae

paul silvester

uk special operations network

vaughan baker
mark channer

colin pope
bramweeks

kensai-quantic-nylon-monoxide
jussi korhonen(fin)
mo denim co c s/r gren(ita)

3906

DOPE DENIM CO
PRODUCT
OF A HOSTILE ENVIRONMENT

どーぶ
ドープ クローージング リミテッド

1 800 d

conceptual design for the pursuit of excellence

Guido f/s boneless

Hossegor/France

Skate of Mind

Unit 26 Thomas Neal Center, Earlham Street Covent Garden London   Tel: + (44) 0207 836 9060
4 Marlborough Court off Carnaby Street London W1 Tel: + (44) 0207 434 0295

Robin 50/50 180 OUT, OXFORD ST BENCHES

04 03 02 01

08 07 06 05

LON

regent's
park

OFF
MAP

euston road

middlesex
hospital

regent's park

st james's
park

victoria street

belgrave road

vauxhall
bridge road

victoria station

the river thames

A.EUSTON BANKS

A.EUSTON BANKS

B.KINGS CROSS RAILS

C.SOAS STUFF

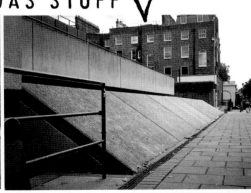

C.SOAS GAP 2 BLOCK

D.RUSSEL SQUARE

D.UNFRIENDLY RESIDENTS

E.GASWORKS HIP

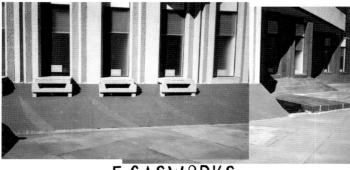

E.GASWORKS

F.DAFT WAVE

G.BRICK BANKS

H.ST PAULS STEPS

I.KNOBBED

I.KNIGHTRIDER STEPS & STUFF

J.THINGY & STEPS

K.CHALKY BLOCKS

L.PISSY RAIL

M. CURVY BLOCK & STEPS

N. FLAT BARS

O. MONUMENT GAP

∧ P. MOORGATE \

P. MOORGATE STEPS

. ORANGE STREET LEDGE

R.STEPS

S.BLOCK

∧ U.PARLIAMENT SQUARE ∧

Y.BANK THINGS⬚ROUGH⬚   **V.BIG BEN ROAD GAP**

Y. VICTORIA BENCHES

AA. VICCY STEPS

AA. HANDRAIL

AA. VICCY KICKER

Z. GAP

Z. DEEP SECRETS

AB. CARPARK KICKER

AB. OVER BAR

AB. SHELL
CENTRE

AB. SHELL DOUBLE

AB. SHELL LEDGE

AB. SHELL SLAPPY

AC. ABOVE BANKS

Λ AC.SOUTHBANK

AC.THE SEVEN

AC.THING

AD.TOTAL BUST BUT LOOK FUN

AC.SOUTHBANK Λ

AC.HIP AND GAP OVER STAIRS

AE.GLASS HANDRAIL

AF.BLOCK STUFF

AG.BLACK BLOCK

AH.METAL BENCHES

AH.LONDON BRIDGE

AH.PLATFORM

AI.METAL EDGE

AI.BAR STUFF

AJ.BANK BLOCK

AK.FLAT BARS

L.LOADS MORE HERE   AN.METAL BLOCK

M.UP UP
DOWN
DOWN >

∧ AP.HAMMERSMITH ☐NEAR A CHURCH☐

AP.
MEANWHIL
ONE
TURN LEFT
OUT OF
WESTBOURI
PARK TUBE

AO.STOCKWELL
BRIXTON TUBE
TURN RIGHT THEN
LEFT AT NEXT CROSSROAD
<

AR.ROMFORD⬚£££££
V

⬚SPOTS NOT SHOWN⬚
AO.CHURCH HANDRAIL

BLUEPRINT
FELLOWSH

PERPETUATING
BRITISH SKATEBOARDING

35

JANET

RE-AL·
BRIGHTON

JASON

7 DUKES LANE 01273 325658

A.SEA FRONT GAP

A.PLATFORM LEDGI

A.VERT RAMP

A.PADDLING RAIL

A.EYEBALL WHEELIES

A.POSSIBLE

D.SOCIAL STEPS

E.AMEX

TON

E. AMEX

H. RAILS

I. LEVEL [MEETING SPOT]

L. MORE CAREFUL PLANNING

. MARINA [MORE]

[SPOTS NOT SHOWN]
B. CHURCHILL SQUARE
C. SLIPKNOT STATUE
G. PEPPERPOT LEDGE
M. TRANNY POND IN WINTER
J&K. DOWNHILLS

LEsSoN OnE
EstAB▢iSH
THe N▲ME
NYL◯N!

FAT MAMAS

5 SYDNEY STREET
BRIGHTON
BN1 4EN

01273 685110

www.fatmamas.co.uk

BORED SKATEBOARD
SHOP. ELM GROVE.
SOUTHSEA 02392426
388

SOUT

Po
CIT

It is an offenc
skateboards,
rollerblades o
device
The War M

MAXiMUM PENALTY UPC

CONTACT CITY RA
MOBILE NUMBER

N

N

A.PYRAMIDS

.PYRAMIDS STEPS

∧
H.GUILD
<HALL

H.GUILDHALL

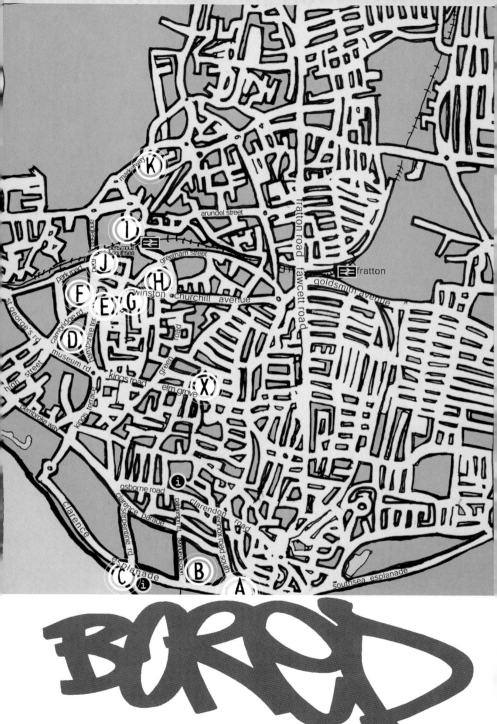

SKATEBOARD SUPPLIES, SOUTHSEA.

D. NICE
CHIP

H. GUILDHALL RAILS

H. KNOBBED

H. NASTY RAIL

H. GUILDHALL

I. STEEP BANKS   YOU FIND IT

J. POLY BANKS □MAD LINES□

J. POLY BANKS

□SPOTS NOT SHOWN□
B. SKATEPARK
C. WALLS STEPS & BLOCKS
E. MINGING BANK 2 WALL
F. PULLMAN FLATBARS
G. DOGSHIT BANKS
K. TRICORN CENTRE
DISUSED SHOPPING CENTRE
□GET BUILDING□

THE DOPE SHOP

established since yesterday
a one stop shop for the
open all hours
mentally equipped

dope clothing **dope**

F SU

nylon

+ other top quality brands

www. **thedopeshop**.co.uk

beat

off beat sportz Ltd
established 1984

186 Above Bar, Southampton, SO14 7DW   Tel: 02380 330600
Unit 3, Upper Wote Street, Basingstoke, RG21 1NE   Tel: 01256 461960
Mailorder: Student discount:
www.offbeatsportz.co.uk

Electrolysis
and
Red Face Veining
Now available
Bookings on (03) 8063 3077

SOUTHA

A. CIVIC STEPS & LEDGE

B. STUPID DOUBLE FLIGHT

B. BBC STEPS

D. STEPS

C. BOARDSLIDE

E. TRAIN STATION DROP IN

Roller Skating, Skate Boarding and all Ball Games are Prohibited in this and every other Southampton City Council Car Park.

MPTON

BEST

F.BANK
DODGY RUN UP

H.CURVY LEDGE

I.NICE FLAT BARS

J.BANK 2 BAR

L.WOODEN BLOCK

O.ROOF GAP
DROP THING

O.STEPS

O.DOUBLEKINK

R.GAP 2 ROAD & RAILS

V.LOADS MORE HERE   S.MAD BANK THING

T.PADDLING POOL NEAR COWHEARDS PUB

[SPOTS NOT SHOWN]   M.STEPS & RAILS   U.GAS RAIL
G.WEST QUAY BUMPS   N.FLAT BARS
K.NICE ROAD GAP   P.TRAMP BANKS

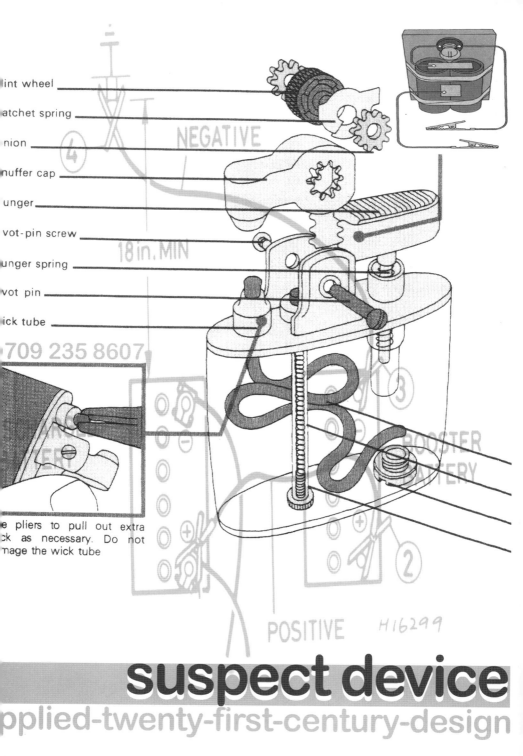

int wheel

atchet spring

nion

nuffer cap

unger

vot-pin screw

unger spring

vot pin

ick tube

NEGATIVE

4

18 in. MIN

709 235 8607

e pliers to pull out extra
ck as necessary. Do not
nage the wick tube

BOOSTER
BATTERY

3

2

POSITIVE   H16299

suspect device
pplied-twenty-first-century-design

96   00   9

88   97   9

01   97   9

www.flatspot.com   10 Whimple Street   Plymouth   01752 22221

flatspot

PLYM

HOE STREET

OUTH

< G.SEA FRONT ⋀

H.CURVY LEDGES

H.AND THESE

H.CARS DRIVE ROUND THESE ⋀

J.PAVILLION BANK 2 WALL >

D.INDOOR BLOCK

L.PIZZA RAILS

M.COPTHORNE LEDGES

N.MONEY CENTRE RAIL

N.LEDGE

O.DOUBLE KINK

FUCK 'EM IF THEY CAN'T TAKE A JOKE

Photo by percy dean

PENZ

ANCE

```
this is th end of the world
this is th end of the world
this is th end of the world
this is th end of the world
this is th end of the world
this is th end of the world
this is th end of the world
this is th end of the world
this is th end of the world
this is th end of the world
this is th end of the world
this is th end of the world

this is th end of the world
this is th end of the world
this is th end of the world
this is th end of the world
this is th end of the world
this is th end of the world
this is th end of the world
```

OTHER SOUTH

TOTNES ☐NEAR TRAIN STATION☐

YATE ☐JUST OUTSIDE BRISTOL☐

TRURO
☐PLAYING PLACE☐

Alphanumeric™

ENVIRON**MENTAL** PROTECTION COMPANY

ALTEC HOUSE
27 AINTREE RD
PERIVALE
MIDDLESEX
UB6 7PL
T +44 (0)208. 997. 4378
F +44 (0)208. 998. 9119

email: alan@purplepin.com

KAREEM CAMPBELL
SPENCER FUJIMOTO
FORREST KIRBY
JAIME REYES
TODD JORDAN
COLT CANNON
TORU YOSHIDA
JEREMY JONES
JEREMY BAYE
BRANDON BYBEE
JORDAN MENDENHALL
LEN HIGA
MARK BREWSTER
JUN JO
JERRY BAGLEY
JOHN RATTRAY

Business As Usual

BRIGADE

Danny Wainwright

ACDONALD · SARMIENTO · MACHNAU · WAINWRIGHT

SKATEPARKS

DUNDEE
THE FACTORY.44 BLINSHALL STREET.
   TEL..01382 907 117
LIVINGSTONE [OUTDOOR]
   HEAD FOR TOWN CENTRE.NEAR ALMONDVALE SHOPPING CENTR
STOCKTON ON TEES
APE SKATE.MARTINET ROAD.THORNABY.STOCKTON
   TEL..01642 764 114
REDCAR
R KADE SKATEPARK.MAJUBA ROAD.REDCAR.CLEVELAND
   TEL..01642 483 520
BOLTON
BONES SKATEPARK.GILMORE LANE.DEANE.
   TEL..01204 392 939
STOCKPORT
BONES SKATEPARK.CANAL STREET.STOCKPORT.CHESHIRE
   TEL..0161 480 8118
LIVERPOOL
RAMPWORX.1[]3 LECKWITH ROAD.NETHERTON.
   TEL..0151 525 3330
CHESTER
THE BONE YARD.TATTEN HALL WORKS.TATTEN HALL RD.
   TEL..01829 770 771
SHEFFIELD [OUTDOOR]
   SEE SHEFFIELD
SHEFFIELD
THE HOUSE.BARDWELL RROAD.NEEPSEND
   TEL..0114 2490 055
DERBY
STORM.COLOMBO STREET.DERBY
   TEL..01332 201 768
KIDDERMINSTER
ROLL N RIDE.STADIUM CLOSE
   TEL..01562 747 040

IF THE PARK HAS
A PHONE NUMBER
THAT MEANS YOU
HAVE TO PAY

⬜SKATEPARKS⬜

WOLVERHAMPTON
WARPED SKATEPARK.
   TEL..01902 453 634
NEWPORT
SK8 EXTREME.HERBERT RD.
   TEL..01633 265 709
CARDIFF
RHYMEY.RIVERBRIDGE.
   TEL..02920 450 359
BRISTOL ⬜OUTDOOR⬜
BEDMINSTER..DEAN LANE
   SEE BEDMINSTER
BRISTOL
SK8 & RIDE.74 AVON ST.
   TEL..0117 907 9995
PETERBOROUGH
Y2SK8.TOWERMEAD IND EST.FLETTON HIGH ST.
   TEL..01733 358 228
NORTHAMPTON
RADLANDS.STUDLAND RD.
   TEL..01604 792 060
HARROW ⬜OUTDOOR⬜
   SEE HARROW
LONDON
PLAYSTATION.60 ACKLAM RD.LADBROKE GROVE
   TEL..0208 969 4669
LONDON ⬜OUTDOOR⬜
   MEANWHILE.SEE LONDON
LONDON ⬜OUTDOOR⬜
ROMFORD SEE LONDON.UPPER RAINHAM RD.ESSEX
   TEL..01708 474 429

KENT
REVOLUTION.OAKWOOD IND EST.
DANE VALLEY RD.BROADSTAIRS.
   TEL..01843 860 707
PORTSMOUTH⬜OUTDOOR⬜
SEE PORTSMOUTH.SOUTHSEA SKATEPARK
   TEL..02392 825 005
SAILSBURY
CHURCHILL GARDENS
MOUNT HAWK
GOVER WATER WORKS.TRURO
   TEL..01209 890 705

NOTES

DEAR SPOTS...

IF BY THIS POINT YOU FEEL EXASPERATED EXCITED ☐ LET DOWN
☐ PUT OFF ☐ YOUR SPOT MISSING
☐ DIFFERENT RULES APPLIED ON YOUR VISIT
☐ YOU DISCOVERED A NEW SPOT
PLEASE MAIL ALL YOUR OUTPOURINGS ☐ SHOTS AND MAPS TO US AND
NEXT TIME WE WILL DO OUR BEST....

☐ I FOUND THE GUIDE USEFUL AND AM PROUD TO HAVE IT.
I LIKE THE PICTURES BUT THE SPOTS ARE TOO MEAN FOR ME.

☐ ARMCHAIR ENTHUSIAST HAS NICE STEPS NEARBY.

☐ PISSED MY SPOT AND FACE ARENT IN IT AND I SKATE MORE
THAN HIM AND HES IN IT.

I ENCLOSE ☐ SPOT ☐ MOAN
☐ MAP ☐ PICTURES
☐ MUMS LETTER ☐ MOREINFO

THANKS...
NAME....
ADDRESS..
E-MAIL

□SPOTS□
PO BOX 84
BRIGHTON
BN1 4WS

DEAR SPOTS...

IF BY THIS POINT YOU FEEL EXASPERATED EXCITED [ ] LET DOWN
[ ] PUT OFF [ ] YOUR SPOT MISSING
[ ] DIFFERENT RULES APPLIED ON YOUR VISIT
[ ] YOU DISCOVERED A NEW SPOT
PLEASE MAIL ALL YOUR OUTPOURINGS [ ] SHOTS AND MAPS TO US AND
NEXT TIME WE WILL DO OUR BEST....

[ ] I FOUND THE GUIDE USEFUL AND AM PROUD TO HAVE IT.
I LIKE THE PICTURES BUT THE SPOTS ARE TOO MEAN FOR ME.

[ ] ARMCHAIR ENTHUSIAST HAS NICE STEPS NEARBY.

[ ] PISSED MY SPOT AND FACE ARENT IN IT AND I SKATE MORE
THAN HIM AND HES IN IT.

I ENCLOSE [ ] SPOT   [ ] MOAN

[ ] MAP   [ ] PICTURES

[ ] MINS LETTER   [ ] MORDINGS

THANKS...
NAME.....
ADDRESS...

☐SPOTS☐

PO BOX 84

BRIGHTON

BN1 4WS

DEAR SPOTS...

IF BY THIS POINT YOU FEEL EXASPERATED EXCITED ☐LET DOWN
☐PUT OFF ☐YOUR SPOT MISSING
☐DIFFERENT RULES APPLIED ON YOUR VISIT
☐YOU DISCOVERED A NEW SPOT
PLEASE MAIL ALL YOUR OUTPOURINGS ☐SHOTS AND MAPS TO US AND
NEXT TIME WE WILL DO OUR BEST...

☐ I FOUND THE GUIDE USEFUL AND AM PROUD TO HAVE IT.
☐ I LIKE THE PICTURES BUT THE SPOTS ARE TOO MEAN FOR ME.

☐ ARMCHAIR ENTHUSIAST HAS NICE STEPS NEARBY.

☐ PISSED MY SPOT AND FACE ARENT IN IT AND I SKATE MORE
THAN HIM AND HES IN IT.

I ENCLOSE ☐ SPOT ☐ MOAN
☐ MAP ☐ PICTURES
☐ MUMS LETTER ☐ MORE INFO

THANKS...
NAME....
ADDRESS...

☐SPOTS☐

PO BOX 84

BRIGHTON

BN1 4WS

CHEERS

OT TO SAY A MASSIVE THANK YOU TO EVERYONE WHO HAS LET ME
LEEP ON THEIR FLOOR BED KITCHEN BATHROOM CAR SOFA
HALF IN HALF OUT THE FRONT DOOR TOILET BACK GARDEN OVER
HE PAST SEVEN YEARS I AM TRULY GRATEFUL FOR YOUR HOSPITALITY.

LSO I WANT TO BIG UP THE WHOLE DOPE POSSE FOR GUIDING ME THROUGH
HE MADNESS OF MAKING THIS GUIDE AND SHOWING ME WHAT INPUT REALLY IS.

AVE DREADS FOR DOING COVENTRY FOR ME AND NOT ME FOR NOT HAVING
NOUGH PAGES TO PUT IT IN.
AZEL DONALDSON FOR THE SHEFFIELD PARK PHOTOS.
EROME FROM WALES FOR TAKING ALL THE BLURRED WALES PORTRAITS ON
OMEONE ELSES DODGY CAMERA HA HA.
ARK CHURCHILL FOR THE MUCH NEEDED EXTRA SOUTHAMPTON FACES BUT
HERES DON.
N FOR FUCKING UP TWO LOTS OF PHOTOS OF HIS MINI RAMP IN PENZANCE
UT IT DOES LOOK GOOD.

LL THE PEOPLE WHO WENT OUT OF THEIR WAY TO GET ME PHOTOS OF UK
DERS IN THEIR ADVERTS COZ THAT S WHO THE KIDS CAN RELATE TO IF
OU THINK ABOUT IT.

Y GIRLFRIEND FOR PUTTING UP WITH ME.

ND A GIGANTIC FUCK YOU TO ANYONE WHO MADE IT HARDER FOR ME TO DO THIS.